YELLOW

Poetry for an Abundant Earth

by

Dr. Majadi Baruti

ISBN: 978-1-365-35949-1

Library of Congress Control Number: 2024926769

Table of Contents

Epigraph..Page 6

Preface..Page 7

Acknowledgements ....Page 9

Marigold

Gently Placed..Page 11

Kudzu...Page 12

A Love Like This....................................Page 14

Cragged Stone...Page 17

Ellipses..Page 17

New Earth..Page 19

To Be Held By Tree................................Page 21

Indigeneity..Page 23

So Much Color.......................................Page 23

On The Ways of Being With Earth........Page 26

Dahlia

Seas..Page 30

This Joyous Light................................Page 32

Murph's Anarchist Guerrilla Garden....Page 34

Life, Death, Flowers.............................Page 38

Of Deepest Dreams...............................Page 39

Holy...Page 40

Holy Too...Page 41

Soft...Page 42

Potatoes...Page 43

Yam..Page 44

On Dichotomy.......................................Page 45

Saffron

Africa's Yellow Love ....Page 47

HER Oak ....Page 48

Flower On My Chest ....Page 49

This Morning's Love ....Page 50

Call To Dirt..Page 51

We Who See Heaven ....Page 53

Flowers, Poems and ....Page 55

Our Pretty Babies ....Page 56

Conversations with Devi ....Page 57

but umm, fly butterfly.........................Page 58

Sunflower

Were I to Cross a Piece of Continent...Page 60

Something Softly Said........................Page 62

This Will Be Enough............................Page 63

Been Cold..Page 64

Tree Spirits..Page 66

In The Sun...Page 68

Love Warriors and Other....................Page 69

Roses, Lilies ....Page 70

Paint My Blackened and Singed.........Page 71

Be The Beautiful Stream ....Page 72

Rose Quartz..Page 73

There is Only Abundance...................Page 75

Coda

"When we love the earth, we are able to love ourselves more fully."

bell hooks

Preface

The fossil fuel industry, banks, corporations, and politicians need to go. As part of the historic climate and environmental justice fight, this has been a long and arduous battle for me, my comrades, and thousands of others. Alabama, Mississippi, Georgia, Puerto Rico, Ohio, Washington, DC, North Carolina, and New York are also fighting these oppressive systems. I've been mostly involved as a man of faith, and as a cleric, but I feel I haven't engaged in it as fully as I could. I've been approaching it with what I've heard called "righteous indignation".

This feeling is rooted in the social injustices I see and experience as a Black Man who loves BIPOC Women and Kids with all his heart. Besides the Earth, I love flowers, trees, animals, air, soil, sunlight, and of course the water. Those loves intersect in my heart as I deal with Climate Change...it brings anger, rage, grief, torment. But that's not the only way I do it. This righteous indignation must side with preaching, teaching and counseling on the beauty and abundance of our Earth.

The set of poetry I want to offer here in Yellow is something of a prayer to the goodness and abundance of planet Earth. Our planet has been home to millions of species, we have been through hundreds of changes and shifts, but the beauty and mostly the abundance has always been present. This prayer I offer you is in the form of poetic verse. Poetry about the planet and about love and the sensuality of love. I see these poems as bits of evidence of how the Great Mother grants us this abundance.

May your mornings be filled with HER grace, may your mondays be filled with HER abundance. There is no lack here on the planet. What we experience are those who create situations of lack. Let those of us of truth and faith behave differently. Let us walk in all that SHE grants us, let our hearts be moved to feed those who hunger, those who thirst, to house those without a home. There's abundance on Mother's Earth, in the way of SHE of 10,000 names by 10,000 names

.

Acknowledgements

I give praise and honor to the Great Mother, who is for me one and the same as the Great Spirit. I give honor to water, fire, air and earth. I give honor to seed, soil and the grace of my African ancestors who were workers in soil. I acknowledge the ancestry of my Devi, my Woman, her Afro-Indigeneity, her love and grace with me, her life saving skills, her medicine.
This work was written on the land of the Wenrohron people, a sovereign people later subsumed by the Haudenosaunee often called the Iroquois Confederacy. I acknowledge their existence in this space and the blessings of their legacy in food and flowers I grow and care for. I acknowledge the ancestors and all of my children, grandchildren and children yet to come. May the Earth's abundance flow for all.

Rev. Dr. Majadi Baruti

Marigold

Gently Placed

Having decided to gently
take this to the next moment
my lips met HER everything
and blessed be the waters that spew forth blessed be
the soil upon which SHE stands
blessed be the air that circles HER children
Blessed be the fire that is HER heart

Kudzu

I am the tiller of the soil,
the caretaker of worms,
I am a child of flowers and food.
My hands are getting mangled,
gnarled
like the tangles of Kudzu,
the sweat of my brow is what is
irrigating this dry Earth for now,
my heart beats in profound
rhythm of Sunflowers and the
coming of Marigold
my friends and I
are accomplices in creating
something beautiful
something wrong
because the enemy likes ugly
I eat of HER well
and drink of HER flesh
I will feed children
build home
and teach, teach ancestral ways
I am neither backwards
nor uncivilized, I am neither
sharecropper nor slave

I am the tiller of the soil
Black,
Brown
gnarled

hands
and love twisted
forever twisted
in wind and rain

A love like this (Dedicated to Earth Warriors, Martin Sostre and Geraldine Pointer)

A love like this does not fold, spindle or mutilate
Its dimensions are not flat nor bloated with hubris
not even upside down,vertical, nor horizontal
It holds no space and is absolutely without time
This love does not run on a diagonal
Straight lines nor can it be lined up
It is neither abstract nor tangible.
Expressionist, Impressionist
This love is not oils nor pastels
It is however charcoal Black
and the Brown flesh
Of Baobab, the red blood of ancestral legacies
Splashing against the walls of eternality
And there is nothing
It cannot be

A love like this will never
ever be featured at your bullshit art museums
It will never make it to your
Top pop 40,
Nor play in football stadiums that gentrify
Black communities
Nor will it be found mulling about
on swanky stanky
Alcohol drenched corners of Elmwood Avenue
A love like this is a lonely hobo seeking to establish
Freedom as a home
Liberation as a vehicle
Driven just to drive these damn oppressors into a
Brick wall

A love like this
Has always been self aware
As revolutionary, motivating and educating
warping and bending time
Doing the improbable
Being the impossible
and absolutely unconquerable

A love like this love cannot be imprisoned
Incarcerated institutionalized
Pushed to the edges of railroad tracks
Landfills, trash incinerators, cancerous allies
Toxic tunnels, Hazardous Waste,
tractor trailer traffic,
intense noise pollution
"tire dust,"
In politicians whose tongues
Salivate with lies,and propaganda
At the behest of fossil fuel agencies
A love like this is Black, Indigenous Women
Dancing together making it actually rain
A storm of change and transformation
This love is a hijab on a black brown woman
maize under a sweet indigenous girl's hands
Bringing sustenance and sovereignty
It is twerking and ballet at the same time
Understanding that neither contradict and both
Have mothers in Afrika

It is collard greens cornbread
Motherships, connections and
imagining sinking slaves
Ships and shit

a love like like this is
Gumbo, banjo and sweet potatoes
It is freeing all political prisoners
Free Em' All
Free Em' All
A love like this is
Chords of Thelonius Monk, Sarah Vaughn,
Memphis Minnie,
Johnny Shines, Nina Simone,
Clifton Chenier and Rick James
This love is you and i bustin' out of this serious joint

A love like this is bustin loose
A love like this
Is poets speaking a most beautiful black
Verse It is writers
And the written that ain't' been wrote yet
the speaker and the unspeakable
A love like this stands on business
Knowing you cannot stand us
and love us
Like we love ourselves
A love like this is us loving ourselves
despite you wishing we would shut the fuck up
A love like this knowing this
We will never be quiet
Because if we did the world would die

Cragged Stone

there will always
be flowers
and wind and trees
let us not
forget
the wonder of trees
rivers racing and crashing
smoothing the cragged stone soul of me as soil
turned leaves and cool grass some of them tall
some of them are fat
some of them holding secrets thorns and fairies
then there will always
be
flowers
this will be enough

Ellipses

This morning....
heck every morning now,
I am thankful for.....sunlight
the blue of day, the warmth of
endless joy sweetness in
foods from our Earth
blackness in our soil, the possibility
of regeneration LOVE ....
and
ellipses ....

New Earth

there is no poem here
not in this bend of time
and
space
and
moments of introspection
instead
we
are caught in what seems constant death
some of us
have a light
an ase'
a chi'
so strong that we will surpass the death
the death will move over and or through us
we live in flowers
and dreams
visions and timelessness
some of us will keep doing old things
not minding the change in weather
climate
and the coming of gale force winds
some of us are not filled with light
filled with a laughter that fills the emptiness
and gives hope

some of us will not make it
into New Earth
and some of us are filled with light
or are masters of the dark

so we will
be here
to guide
those with an open heart
and those who don't live in their head

To Be Held By Tree

earth,
earth,
earth,
earth,
earth,
earth,
earth,
earth,
earth,
earth,
Earth....
Mother's heartbeat
love

warmth
sustenance
habiliment
Home.
earth,
earth,
earth,
earth,
earth,

to be held by tree and

loved by flowers, to eat of fruit, plump, wet, my mouth quenched, desires met, heart filled, head cooled, feet refreshed in the newness of morning....

my nude brown matching soil and leaf turning colors, I am of HER and SHE is abundance and fulfilling of my every need

earth, earth, earth, earth, earth, earth, earth, earth, earth, earth, earth, earth

Indigeneity

Blood
brown skin in soil
skin
flowers sprouted
a very revolutionary crop
tears
ruby flesh in soil
love growing
an intense tearing asunder
darkness love and
Indigenous skin in soil
food everlasting
a beautiful remembrance
They are tomorrow and yesterday and always and
They are sovereign

So Much Color

my words are peppered with joy and Earth's
color, so much color
she brings
no emptiness
no dreary rain, every drop being an equivalent joy
I am often
unprepared to see her face
giggling
as if a schoolboy of 12
uncontrollable breathing and mirth
running
to
the
phone
when she calls
she brings so much color
sound in abundance
my being a fool
I cry the tears of a clown
court jester
I am a fool
somewhere
between tomorrow
and
her beautiful smile

I became
a Prophet
she remains
a very
very
very
beautiful mystery
especially her Indigenous thighs

On The Ways Of Being With Earth

There is no dichotomy in nature, there are more than just two types of trees, flowers, dogs, moose, and even porcupine. Not only are these species are not in opposition to each other, they actually exist in a circularity and rhythmic way with one another. The predator and prey dynamic is not an oppositional work but one that allows the continuity of life. Only in the extreme insanity of humans can there be such a thing as dichotomy, as vast as the numbers of humans on the planet some 8.5 Billion there are at least as many ways of being. Such is the same for the Earth, for nature, we are of the Earth, part of HER and part of nature.

We are not to be the masters of nature but family with all living things, all sentient life is connected. For that matter we are connected to that which isn't' even perceived as "alive' ' as well. For instance I just went to get some eggs from the local store for my Fiance', I began to think about eggshells and how I use them for composting and putting in the soil around my plants. My heart continuously experiences this as regeneration; Chicken produces eggs, eggs bring full grown chickens, both are used by some beings as food. These beings then produce waste which goes into the Earth, the same Earth and plants therein are eaten by Chickens.

We all know this cycle well, right? We learn about it in school, early on but are we taught the sacredness of this unending cycle? Are we even taught this sacredness in Church, Temple, Masjid, Synagogue ? Are we approaching even the sweetness of the Chicken's egg as part of this divine play? There is the argument on eating meat and meat based products, I myself have been Vegan, Vegetarian, Pescatarian and Omnivorous. I did not find myself in any argument with folks on any side of this. This is humanity as a whole, we are many things and this is fine. The argument is absurd on both sides unless it centers the sacredness of our planet, and truth being told, indigenous folks have it right.

Those of us who live closest to the land and revere the soil and water have it right. Humans have lived as consumers of animal flesh, bone and hair for thousands of years, it was done in thankfulness and gratitude, not for the sake and pursuit of power over but in divine connection with. If we return to this understanding of our holy relationship with all, acquiring only what we need. If we would fill our hearts with giving of ourselves to a type of stewardship of life and death, we will all be fine. Now eat your food and mind your own business.

Dahlia

Seas

We are small streams,

that feed ponds, and tiny rivers,

that bless animals and flowers,

and grasses and trees.

We are small streams

that feed ponds and larger........ rivers ....

that flow most from the topography on

the planet often from South To North

but this direction is determined by the topography

of hills and mountains and stones and sand and

silt and river banks causing the waters to flow downward and

in varied directions....We will meet up at Seas and Oceans at some point.

....these Seas and Oceans teeming with so much life,

literally brings us all life...We are of the Water,

assisted by Fire, Earth and Air....

and so forth but the

waters of of our Great Black Mother's Womb

is consistent,

we are born of Womb

and to Womb we shall return.

Be the beautiful stream that you are and flow unceasing... on your own path.

Ase'

Ase

'Ase'

This Joyous Light

even the scent
of rubber from tires
the hardness of
concrete under my feet.
The cold of glass
spilled garbage ...
This parking lot
this empty building
    boarded up on the front
windows on the side some shattered like our lives
replete with dirty windows
on the back and the
ragged porch ready to splinter.
Homes haunted by lack of investment housing
brutally slaughtered by lack of love,
not love from we who live here certainly
but love from the governments
we elect. We recognize they
do not love us
  still our children play amongst the flowers in the
grass that still resides here. At essence, our children
play amongst themselves as they are flowers
We are an impossible flower.
Our children still run and play Tag
Or hide-and-go-seek.
Our children are still smiling
even in the filth of pollution
from the air soil water
    Even with the dollar stores used as food. Our
children are still laughing

They are dying, but they are not dead yet. We are dying, but we are living simultaneously at the edge of death.
We are all laughing.
Nothing to do but cry
crying to laugh.
Hoping to laugh
hoping for joy
pushing for grace,
        we are still laughing because
We are an improbable flower
we are not
dead and we will not die.
We will live on in the grass
as flowers blooming growing from nothingness.
We are an impossible bouquet
they try to kill us
but we are flowers
and seed
and soil
and sun
and wind
and water
and love
and love
and love

Murph's Anarchist Guerrilla Garden
(Requiem for Murph)

What a question
were they not a tree?
one that smiles, and teaches us
to grow
without cease, without end
were they not a tree
knotty hair and so much more rooted
then all of us?
teaching us to root ourselves
in
earth
and
love
were they not flowers?
and abundant with petals
softness and grace
promising newness and joy
a sip from a bee
a taste from a hummingbird
to spread love through the land
were they not a flower
consuming our thoughts with
the fragrance of revolution

capturing our vision
teaching us to sit still
in
patience
and
compassion
were they not a fire?
the fire that kept us warm
and knowing
and safe
and blessed to cook our food
our food needed for our transformation
and to burn away
the filth of this machine world
the fire being for purification
teaching us to be perpetual in
our burning
were they not a fire?
burning
scorching
leaving nothing but truth
and enemy towers for us
to dance upon
drink upon
in

laughter
and
knowing
were they not holy herbs?
to burn
to burn
to get us all intoxicated on life
and freedom
so high
so cosmic
as to kiss clouds
excusing us while we kissed the sky
yet so grounded
that we
would no longer hallucinate
but freedom would be real
and very real
and very very real
and so real that Afrofuturism
was the becoming
and the Lorde's work
was here and very very real
and SONGs would be sung
and SONGs would be sung
on hills made of dynamite

and hills so high that they
taught us to become Highlanders
and our Southern Ways would
become more clear
so clear that we could see past
the enemies coal ash
and blackface
and bourgeois dances
and lies told in progression
one after the other faded
faded and our friend, our dear friend
our comrade, our compatriot
our Detonator brought the
most incendiary love
we could feel
and were they not incendiary?
and herbs, and flowers and trees
and did they not teach us
that our way is love
so that all we have to do is
lean in ?

Life, Death, Flowers

Words bent around trees
    trees bent around lust
reality bent around them both
unspoken words taking flight
        but the happening,
the bending and twisting of their possible bodies
and impossible pull towards
one
another remained
the happening was there
neither questioned it but remained foolish
smiles
conversations of life, death, flowers
smiles
the pulling of sacral energy
the potential bending and twisting of their possible
nudeness
yet the crying out not met
because
they
were
both
pretending that none of this is true

Of Deepest Dreams

of deepest dreams
 and writhing in
ecstasy,
      the deepest surviving flowers
honey can be found in the most
 concrete spaces,
glass,
pipes,
steel, metal, creaking bending
they will
because of this honeyed position
stay in
a loving and a
sweet place
one in which abundance
is perpetual

Holy

Holy of Holies....
grow flowers,
grow herbs for them,
honor the Moth
for our children, these future dancers in puddles
puddles and oh yes, mud
Holy of Holies
help us to be as children
current dancers in mud and splashes of water
let us remember tadpoles and frogs
and how nice the rain is
even if we can't play outside
we can dream inside
Oh Holy of Holies
help us laugh as herbs heal
and smile as flowers
and remember the softest of things

Holy Too

Today I feel blessed
that LOVE
did not put
an executioner's costume on
and try to kill me
this time...... I mean
this time
instead
she
is wearing
yellow
and holy books come out of her
mouth
but
then
again
I am a poet
the only thing I know are
Juniper, mint, hyacinth and such
words filled with microbes
To grow

Soft

The softest of mornings, autumn, Buffalo
next to me, this lovely caramel, sacred bedchamber
dim lighting at morning, thoughts on silken ascot and
how
I might look in them
SHE is my wondrous love
something soft on this softest of mornings
I am still pondering the color of HER skin......flesh
I am settling on caramel...i am wondering how long i
might be here
She inspires ....yellow....the brightness of morning sun
The brilliance of Coneflowers and the joy of Canna
Lilies
She inspires.....yellow

Potatoes

Planted potatoes today,
turned over grass and soil
which was difficult with all the
Red Clay here in Alabama,
used some compost,
compost is Decay and Death for those that don't
know
for from Death comes Life everlasting,
SHE our beautiful planet
gave me compost by
regenerating herself
our ends of fruit and vegetables
and grass shavings and fallen leaves and in return
SHE the wondrous Earth
will give us more food!
This is all, you give and SHE gives
true reciprocity
lovely circles of love
to love is an act of giving
to give is an act of love

Yam

.....there are those of us
who have decided
to be abundance
to become fat with love
there are those of us
who have made up our minds
to live by our hearts
there are those of us
who have embraced this moment
as moist as soil
we are becoming flowers
and eggplant
tomatoes and swiss chard
we are told we are what we eat
oh how lovely we taste
as sage and purple basil
me....well my friends, I am a
Yam of course.

There is no dichotomy in nature, there are more than just two types of trees, flowers, dogs, moose, porcupine even. Not only are these things not in opposition to each other, Roses do not go "Against" Daffodils. Only in the extreme insanity of humans can there be such a thing as dichotomy, the suggestion that there are only two types of political parties is just as insane. The potential for political thought is as vast as the numbers of humans on the planet.

Now.....go outside and play

Saffron

Africa's Yellow Love

how
dare we discard Africa
as if beauty is not at
her
wondrous foundation
what of yellow, Hmmm?
What of yellow?
and the wonderment to be found
there.
splashes of yellow against
love
and sweet scents
how dare we forget
Yellow ?

HER Oak

And there SHE was
my lover
Earthen scented, flowered so abundantly
all volcanic of spirit
So I hugged one of HER Oak
and the orgasmic throes of light
that shot through my body
let me know
that indeed
SHE is God

Flower On My Chest

SHE moves as if dove feathers
and flowers were HER first name,
SHE spins ever so cosmically
slightly towards me and I..
..ascend...
tonight, I am in HER days,
at Day, I am all in HER night,
when the Dawn comes, so does love,
I have a flower on my chest
whoever said love is pain
is dead from being brutally beaten
by having none at all
and they have forgotten
flowers die but their seeds
are not dead

This Morning's Love

under here
blanket, her flesh
soft, warm, brown
pretty flower that she is
this morning's love
seems a dream
but it is the most yellow of things
soft, warm, sunshine even in
the grey or is it gray
of this morning sky
this morning's love shines
heat of her caramel body
healing my minds flame
cooling the heat from my heart
as men destroy our earth
hubris arrogance and evil be damned
this morning's love
is just knowing
that she in her caramel brown
brings shine
brightness
hope and possibility
the prettiest flower is her kiss
the sweetest honey
her smile
dawn breaks
this morning's love has me

Call To Dirt

call to dirt
sweat
work of worth
the dying things please me
brown and withered leaves vine
and the cavernous dark of death
thank Goddess there is no romance
here
I have no time for that bullshit
cow shit
horse shit
chicken shit
give it all to me
let it turn death
into living matter
heat
sweat
the growing of things
bodies healed
hunger pangs and pains fading
away
children playing
Black Mother
loves me and the dirt under my
nails
the children laugh and play
they worked hard
community daughter loves

like no other
caring for the elders and the children of
love
she has had this soup

Sweet Potato and Collards
she is able to laugh
death is composted
just for HER my
daughter
my daughter, my community daughter
there was always abundance
the shit in HER life
composted
and now some whiskey
then to sleep
and we will sleep well

We Who See Heaven

in the eyes of our children
and feel peace shake the earth in want
and desire
to be
present
evermore
we are love's greatest warriors
we who experience the trees
flowers, and butterflies
in the eyes of our children
and are moving as seed in the wind
through the next portal
and desire
to be
present
in love evermore
we are love's greatest shaman

we who see heaven
in the eyes of our children
and feel peace shake the earth in want
and desire
to be
present
evermore

we are love's greatest warriors
we who experience the trees
flowers, and butterflies
in the eyes of our children
and are moving as seed in the wind
through the next portal
and desire
to be
present
in love evermore
we are love's greatest shaman

Poems, Flowers and....

Even
in
loss
grief
loneliness
hurt
pain
making me soil
consuming me as if i were water
they are here
flowers and this butterfly that my love says to me
" it is here for you"
these poems find me
make me love them
put themselves in my verbiage
make me whole
cut me into infinitesimal pieces
make me love them
make me them
make of me what they will

Our Pretty Babies

they are seeds of thought
hope
and remedies to heartache
lake charles babies
chicago babies
toronto and birmingham babies
these pretty water babies
dancing
as if flying babies
hair flowing in wind
laughter babies
even unborn they are here babies
as if in dream form
just the want
the desire to have them
is a type of love
just the desire for these pretty babies
makes me love
this woman more
these chicago and lake charles babies
cowboy and b-boy babies
smiling babies
cornbread babies
sunflower babies
sunflower and tomato red babies
red twin babies
our pretty little flower babies.

Conversations with Devi

SHE who has
come from a mist
a mist that I could not peer through
but felt
deeply
as if a whisper and a promise were there
now meeting
   HER honeyed sunshine and contours
the softness therein
SHE brings with HER religion and
new possibilities......SHE brings with HER
all forms of connections to Turtle Island
and flowers
oh these flowers
HER flower, one not yet seen and tasted only in thought
and herbs, and children, the laughter of children around
HER
Saturday mornings and a gathering of fruit
a gathering
of
fruit

but umm...fly butterfly

but umm.....fly
but ummm....fly butterfly
with all your song
and sway in the wind
float on float on as if
no-one were present
as if no one was there
as if you and I were alone
butterfly
what more do we need but this
soft forever

Sunflower

Were I to cross a piece of the continent

Were I to cross a piece of the continent
only to see
her smile
one might think me in
love and one might
think me insane
and here I am
reaching into the deepest part
of yellow
finding nothing but a passport a yellow
paged notepad
poems spoken to a mist
and a mystery
a miracle
and a desire to be happy
a sharp sharpie
the sharpest kind
the one that allows
poetry to be written on a yellow paged
notebook
The kind
of sharpie that allows a Cocoa covered
man once shrouded in smog
asphyxiating
on
depression
to come from such somewhat scathed
and so much worse for the wear

Now comes this
offering of yellow
yellow
and coconut milk
healing
and her soft hands

Something Softly Said

something softly said
a moan
the sound of leaves shifting about
a whisper of love
as if gems had voice
something spoken
as if in haste but with care
a name
their names
in the night sky told
to deities, the trees
the rain
their lips, and something softly
kissed
their curves and contoured pleasure
embraced
by both geometry and orgasm
something screamed
an explosion of lust
as if incendiary in their fucking
a bomb
the bomb
their ecstasy
softly spoken, minds blown
hearts entwined
in water and honey

This Will Be Enough

The push-the-pull
the bend
the twist
the turn
the hope
the joy
this will be enough
after our revolt today
our sweet potato pies
that Big Mama makes
For us to share each
Time she does so she makes more than enough
because there is always more than enough
Our push back will be enough our rebellion will be
enough or laughs will be enough our taunts will be
enough are teasing good enough our songs, are
chance, our fight, and yes even our deaths will be
enough we will find a way and that way
Will be enough

Been Cold

Alabama Winter
been cold....blood racing the earth cold
wind stormed cat o' nine tails cold
ripped shoes, trash from the table from Massa'
cold
land sold us to Alabama Power cold
frozen hearts, colonizer grits eating overthrow the
planter
cold
modern day negro overseer in shiny suits well
manicured
souls.....so manicured til' you see the white meat pork
meat
unclean unclean fatter with development incentives
cold

heart watching homeless freeze while you sit and eat
Southern Company 7 course lies with ease

cold

cold

cold you cold man, blood drenched soil slave sweat
cold

whip whizzing in the wind smashing black flesh

ring around the collar hang there til' you take one last holla'

cold

Alabama been cold been told been old Sessions cold old take it all cold all 23 million acres cold trail of tears and call it Cessions cold hell is hot but Alabama is hotter and in the same cold breath Alabama been cold

Alabama been cold

Alabama been cold

But the fire done come now.......and they ain't playin'

It's the People's Revolution for me

Tree Spirits

The Great Mother's Tree Spirits that are speaking to me through dream and embrace are giving warnings, deadly ones. I have now had several dreams wherein Tree Spirits are telling me we are being challenged. Let me say it like this: these are DEADLY warnings, not some cheap commercial with Smokey Bear. This is not an environmental, save the tree type of thing. I have been holding back for a while for fear that I will be thought of as crazy, well, no more. THIS IS IT! If you see garbage, trash on the Earth, pick it up and dispose of it. If you see folks swinging from trees or hurting them in any way, yeah I mean construction companies and all, tell them to stop post-haste. This society has enough buildings, enough banks and grocery stores, we need trees and plants, fruit and vegetables. You must ask yourself are y you participating in a war paradigm that is suicidal? Are you supporting politicians who want to bring progress by progressively killing nature which is of dire necessity for us all to live? The Tree Spirits are pissed to say the least. Indeed they are giving Deadly Warnings. We are called to bring a new way with ancient lineage, one in which true balance can be had, this is the way of the Mother.

In The Sun

In the sun, sunlight
warmth prior to a storm, flowers
to behold
    pretty grasses and clover
my want to be with soil and fruit
compost, and behold those flowers
mint and poppy, sunflowers and tomato
let me toil here
            in this wild, HER wild
HER breath soft and when angry
   the wind sweeping across my cocoa body
my brow drenched with the tears of ancestresses
in the sun, sunlight
      sweltering prior to a storm
Maypop and Pumpkin/Punkin'
                 organized as work of the Goddess
my folks knew HER too
     barefoot to soil, keep me barefoot and harvesting
my hands and heart are here in this dirt
this Alabama dirt
Machete, Pitchfork, Axe.....I am ready to hold this
space

Love Warriors and Other Contradictions

Repeatedly whooping
ass with sweet corn and sassafras
floral memories drawing in oceans of beauty
rivers running south to north
running colonizers backwards
breaking stone and soaking seashore
    love warriors sounding contradictory while
whipping
evil soundly, thrashing it about
even in our non-violence, love will bring
shadow and knock the unrighteous from their feet
flower petals, thorns and such
never quite dying but living evermore
more than seed
we are healing microbes and ashwagandha
jasmine in bloom, the vibrations of soulful mint
and sweetly made love
love's warriors committing no war
but ending it

Roses, lilies

Roses, lilies
and some others are growing
still seemingly against time…
a beautiful expression of the Earth's
love
and my love for HER

Paint My Blackened and Singed Heart

that

she

would and could paint my blackened and singed

heart

yellow

as if some southern sunshine

rested upon me

I can't find words

I choke on them

trying

trying

to not

let this paint chip

and peel

this yellow

that shines on me

her

yellow

Be The Beautiful Stream

We are small streams, that feed ponds, and tiny rivers, that bless animals and flowers, and grasses and trees. We are small streams that feed ponds and larger rivers that flow most from the topography on the planet often from South To North but this direction is determined by the topography of hills and mountains and stones and sand and silt and river banks causing the waters to flow downward and in varied directions....We will meet up at Seas and Oceans at some point.....these Seas and Oceans teeming with so much life, literally brings us all life...We are of the Water, assisted by Fire, Earth and Air....and so forth but the waters of of our Great Black Mother's Womb is consistent, we are born of Womb and to Womb we shall return. Be the beautiful stream that you are and flow unceasing... on your own path.

Ase'

Rose Quartz

In my heart of hearts
all Pink and Rose Quartz
all crystalline and loving
all giving and always present
there is no you and then me
no me and then you, there isn't misery
only the sensual glory of your smile

In my gut there is no fear
of loving you endlessly
there is no shore my feet fear to tread
there is no food I will not give you
with my fingers moist and soaked in oil
I will feed you
In the deepest illness I am present and
waiting on you, in light in dark
I am smiling endlessly and nothing stops this grin
I am Brown Gnome and you Undine
show me the waters I will build you flowers
this we can do forever

you will not need for anything

I live deep in forest realms

hidden by magic a mushroom over my head

a book in my hands, let me read to you

of ancient songs and hymns to lilies in bloom

let me recite poems of sweet rivers screaming Oshun

let me recite a verse in Yemaya prose.

I can dance nude if you like, this I can do

with a mushroom on my head

There is Only Abundance

May the morning be filled with HER grace,
may your midday be filled with HER abundance,
there is no lack here on the planet
of the
Great Black Goddess.
What we experience are those
who create
situations of lack.
Let those of us of
truth and faith
behave differently.
Let us walk in all that SHE grants us, l
let our hearts be moved to feed those who hunger,
those who thirst, to house those without home. On
Mother's Earth, in HER way, in the way of SHE of
10,000 by 10,000 names, there is only abundance.

Coda

In my heart's imagination I have leaped forward into a time when we are not in this Climate Crisis. Will you join me ? Or perhaps indulge with me for a moment on what this might look like ? It is inconceivable for some of us, but for me, dreams are as real as the here and now.

In this future the Climate Crisis has been solved by doing several things and not necessarily in this order. We are centering love, Black, Indigenous Women and children. Not just their voices but also their presence in how the community is structured and how we govern ourselves. In this future Capitalism is being dismantled and the "market" centers the Women and their understanding of cooperative and bartering systems. We are moving towards Earth's regeneration as we grow more than we remove from the planet for food.

We are ceasing our use of fossil fuels after a long fight in some very volatile organizing and activism, numerous arrests and death beyond belief but we won. The children of the Earth defended her with all we could muster, and by any means we found necessary. The age of fossil fuels has ended, the time of the Mother and love are being heralded. We are rematriating all land and water, we have come to realize we must center Mother.
We have Fathers here with us that are nurturing caretakers of all of us, we are bringing new meaning to, "No Child Left Behind"

www.ingramcontent.com/pod-product-compliance
Ingram Content Group UK Ltd.
Pitfield, Milton Keynes, MK11 3LW, UK
UKHW041920190726
13854UKWH00003B/1360

9 781365 359491